Media Law *for* Canadian Journalists

SECOND EDITION

DEAN JOBB

2011
EMOND MONTGOMERY PUBLICATIONS
TORONTO, CANADA

emp

Emond Montgomery Publications Limited
60 Shaftesbury Avenue
Toronto ON M4T 1A3
http://www.emp.ca/highered

Printed in Canada on 100 percent recycled paper.
Reprinted August 2012.

We acknowledge the financial support of the Government of Canada through the Canada Book Fund for our publishing activities.

Acquisitions and development editor: Mike Thompson
Marketing manager: Christine Davidson
Director, sales and marketing, higher education: Kevin Smulan
Supervising editor: Jim Lyons
Copy editor: David Handelsman
Proofreader: Andrew Gordon
Text designers and typesetters: Shani Sohn and Tara Wells
Indexer: Paula Pike
Cover designers: Stephen Cribbin & Simon Evers
Author photo: Kerry Oliver

Library and Archives Canada Cataloguing in Publication

Jobb, Dean, 1958-
Media law for Canadian journalists / Dean Jobb. — 2nd ed.

Includes index.
ISBN 978-1-55239-420-5

1. Mass media—Law and legislation—Canada.   2. Press law—Canada.
3. Journalists—Legal status, laws, etc.—Canada.   4. Criminal law—Canada.
5. Civil law—Canada.   I. Title.

KE2550.J62 2010   343.7109'9   C2010-907044-5
KF2750.J62 2010

Contents